GEO

ABE Concept

ⁱⁱ/₀₂

D0535982

S is for Show Me

A Missouri Alphabet

Written by Judy Young

Illustrated by Ross B. Young

Sleeping Bear Press
310 North Main Street
P.O. Box 20
Chelsea, MI 48118
www.sleepingbearpress.com

Printed and bound in Canada.

10 9 8 7 6 5 4 3 2 1

Library of Congress Cataloging-in-Publication Data
ISBN: 1-58536-026-0

Young, Judy.
S is for show me : a Missouri alphabet / written by Judy Young ; illustrated by Ross Young.
p. cm.
Summary: Various objects, places, people, and animals associated with the state of
Missouri are presented in short rhymes with added commentary and are used to
illustrate the alphabet.

Missouri—Juvenile literature. 2. English language—Alphabet—Juvenile literature.
[1. Missouri—Miscellanea. 2. Alphabet.] Young, Ross, ill.

F466.3 .Y68 2001
977.8—dc21   2001042893

For Brett and Reid
and all the other children of Missouri,
past, present, and future.

J. Y. and R. B. Y

Welcome to the Show Me State.
It's Missouri and I think it's great!
If you'll come along with me
I'll show you Missouri from A to Z.

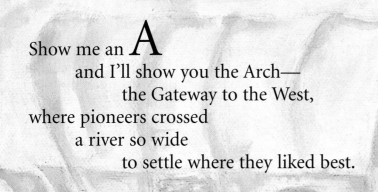

Show me an A
    and I'll show you the Arch—
        the Gateway to the West,
where pioneers crossed
    a river so wide
        to settle where they liked best.

The Gateway Arch at the Jefferson National Expansion Memorial is the tallest monument in the U.S. The Arch towers 630 feet above the banks of the Mississippi River. Completed in 1965, the Arch symbolizes our country's development of the West. Trees planted on the park grounds represent the wilderness the pioneers found. An open area under the Arch represents clearings the settlers made.

Special trams take you to the top of the Arch where you can look out across St. Louis. From there, you can see the Old Courthouse where the famous Dred Scott trials regarding slave rights were held in 1847. Look for Ead's Bridge, the first bridge that crossed the Mississippi River in St. Louis. It's also the world's first steel truss bridge. This bridge allowed the eastern and western railroad systems to join.

There are at least 15 arches in the picture. Can you find them all?

Aa

Big Spring is America's largest single outlet spring. The aqua-blue water gushes out at the base of a cliff. It releases an average of 277 million gallons of water a day. Like all of Missouri's 1,100 springs, the water is very cold. Although it may be clear and inviting, a spring's water quality is greatly influenced by surface conditions. It's important to remember that fertilizers or pesticides used many miles away can seep their way into the spring water.

Springs were so important to the settlers that 66 towns in Missouri have "spring" in their names. Settlers used spring water for drinking, watering livestock, and powering gristmills, which ground corn and wheat into flour. Today, the cold water at some springs is used for trout hatcheries.

This great blue heron is visiting Big Spring. Can you find other visitors?

Show me a B
and we'll stop at Big Spring
where peaceful greens surround
a torrent of water
that sparkles and swirls
as it gushes out of the ground.

Show me a C
and we'll remember the Civil War,
a terrible fight that tore
apart families and friendships
with different views,
ending slavery forevermore.

Cc

When the Civil War broke out, Missouri was a Union slave state. Some felt it should remain in the Union; others thought it should join the Confederacy. Missouri was an important state because of its major shipping routes on the Mississippi and Missouri Rivers. Nathaniel Lyon led the Union in one of the earliest battles in Missouri at Wilson's Creek. He was the first Union general killed in the Civil War. Because of this battle, Missouri remained a Union state. Many soldiers killed at Wilson's Creek are buried at the Springfield National Cemetery, the only national cemetery where Union and Confederate soldiers are buried side by side.

In January 1865, Missouri became the first slave state to abolish slavery. The Lincoln Institute was founded a year later by black soldiers, many of them ex-slaves, who gave their money to educate freed slaves. It is now the Lincoln University in Jefferson City.

Can you point to a Union soldier and a Confederate soldier? You can tell by the color of their uniforms and their flags.

Show me a D
and we'll find dogwood trees
and smell hawthorn's sweet bouquet.
As we walk in the country
in the warm, spring sun,
a bluebird may fly our way.

The flowering dogwood is Missouri's state tree. Its blossoms of four white petals dot the forests in the spring.

If you walk through the woods on an early spring day, you may also smell the sweet scent of the hawthorn blossom, Missouri's state floral emblem. These clusters of white flowers are related to the rose, although they grow on a tree!

Dogwoods and hawthorns provide berries for Missouri's state bird, the Eastern bluebird. It is a symbol of hope and happiness. The bluebird also likes to eat insects. What insects are hiding from these bluebirds? For a while, the number of bluebirds decreased due mainly to loss of habitat. Today many people build nesting boxes to help bluebirds find homes.

Can you find the male? His feathers are brighter in color.

There are 12 bluebirds throughout this book. Can you find them?

Dd

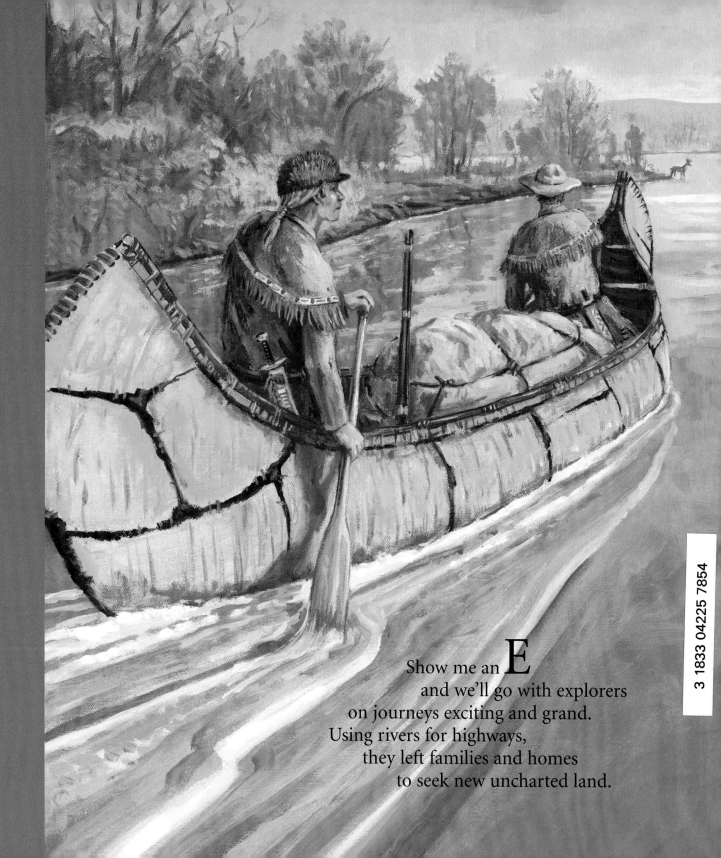

Many famous explorers came to Missouri. In 1673, French explorers Joliet and Marquette canoed down the Mississippi, becoming the first Europeans to set foot in Missouri and to see the Missouri River. La Salle, another French explorer, claimed the Mississippi Valley for France, naming it the Louisiana Territory. In 1803, President Thomas Jefferson of the United States made the Louisiana Purchase, buying the land from France for $15 million. He wanted to learn about this new territory, so in 1804, he hired Lewis and Clark to travel up the Missouri River. Starting from St. Louis, they left on a two-year expedition, exploring all the way to the Pacific Ocean.

Not all expedition leaders were grown-ups. In 1764, Pierre Laclede, a fur trader, wanted a town for his headquarters. He sent 14-year-old Auguste Chouteau as the leader of the building expedition. Chouteau led a 30-man crew up the Mississippi to build the first cabins of St. Louis.

eE

Show me an E
and we'll go with explorers
on journeys exciting and grand.
Using rivers for highways,
they left families and homes
to seek new uncharted land.

The fiddle, Missouri's state musical instrument, is the smallest orchestral string instrument. The fiddle is made of wood. To play it, a bow made with horsetail hairs is slid across its four strings. The strings can also be plucked.

Because it was small, the fiddle was often brought west by fur traders and homesteaders to play in the evenings after the work was done. A famous fiddle, Pa's fiddle, is on display in Mansfield where Laura Ingalls Wilder lived when she wrote the "Little House" books.

Foot-stomping fiddle tunes liven up hoedowns and jamborees. As callers call out the steps, "swing your partner and do-si-do," fiddles set the rhythm for a square dance, Missouri's state dance. A gal and her beau may softly two-step as a fiddle plays the Missouri Waltz, our state song.

Ef

Show me an F
and we'll dance to the fiddle
as its music takes hold of our feet.
Swing to the right,
then pull your girl tight,
step in time to the rhythmical beat.

In the center of Missouri's flag are two grizzly bears holding the Great Seal of Missouri. The bears, once native to Missouri, represent strength and courage. The stars above the bears show that Missouri was the 24th state. There are two mottoes on the flag. "United We Stand, Divided We Fall" tells how important it is to work together. The other, which is in Latin, means "Let the welfare of the people be the supreme law." Why do you think that an eagle and the red, white, and blue bands were chosen to be on our flag?

In 1803, Missouri became a territory of the United States. It became a state on August 10, 1821.

Did you know that there are two ways to pronounce Missouri? Some say "Missour-EE," and others say "Missour-UH." Which way do you say it?

Show me a G
and we'll find grizzly bears
standing bravely by the Great Seal.
As it waves on our flag,
we salute it to show
how proud Missourians' feel.

H h

Show me an H
and we'll watch honeybees
abuzz among the flowers,
gathering pollen,
a dust gold as honey,
filling long summertime hours.

The honeybee is Missouri's state insect. Each bee in a hive has a specific job. There is one queen bee that lays all the eggs. Males, called drones, mate with the queen. The female bees are called workers.

Young workers, called house bees, clean the hive, feed the larvae, and build honeycomb. When they are older, they become guard bees, protecting the hive from intruders. Finally, they become foragers, finding flowers, drinking nectar, and gathering pollen. House bees turn the nectar and pollen into honey, sealing it in the six-sided cells of the honeycomb. They tell other bees where to find flowers by doing a special dance.

Not only do bees make honey, but they also help to pollinate plants so seeds and fruit will grow.

Do you see a crab spider?

Show me an I
    and we'll eat ice cream cones
on a hot summer's day at the fair.
    A winter cold taste
    drips sweet on your tongue;
you can bring it along anywhere.

The first ice cream cone was invented in 1904 at the St. Louis World's Fair. At that time, disposable paper dishes and plastic silverware were not used. Ernest Hamwi thought if ice cream were put in a waffle rolled into a cone, sightseers could take their ice cream with them. These cones, made from Persian waffles, were called "goherettes." It also saved a lot of dishwashing! Other food inventions claimed by the St. Louis World's Fair were iced tea, the hot dog, the hamburger, and toasted ravioli.

One structure that remains from the fair is a walk-through aviary. You can still walk through this "bird cage" to see many colorful birds at the St. Louis Zoo.

Can you find two flamingos, a macaw, a whooping crane, and five ice cream cones?

i
I

Show me a J
and we'll visit Jefferson City
where our state capitol stands.
To honor our state,
let's celebrate
with fireworks, parades, and bands.

Jefferson City is the capital of Missouri. Frequently called Jeff City, it was named after President Thomas Jefferson.

The Missouri State Capitol building sits on a hill overlooking the Missouri River. It houses the Senate, the House of Representatives, and the Governor's offices, as well as other governmental offices. The Missouri State Museum, with displays about state history and resources, is also located in the capitol.

Missourians are proud of the amount of artwork decorating their capitol. Outside are fountains, sculptures, and statues. Inside the capitol numerous paintings reflect the people and history of Missouri. The most famous is a mural painted on the walls of the house lounge by Thomas Hart Benton, a Missouri artist.

J j

Show me a K
        and we'll dig at Kimmswick Bone Beds
    where mastodons roamed the land.
        Early man hunted
    these mighty beasts
with a spear held in his hand.

Skeletal remains of more than 60 mastodons have been found at or near the Kimmswick Bone Beds at the Mastodon State Historic Site. However, what makes this spot even more special is that, in 1979, a Clovis spear point was found in direct contact with a mastodon bone. This is the only place in North America where evidence has been found that man and mastodon lived together 10,000 to 14,000 years ago at the end of the Ice Age.

The mastodons were 10 feet tall at the shoulder, about 20 feet long, and weighed up to six tons. They ate coarse vegetation such as leaves, twigs, and tender parts of trees and shrubs.

Other prehistoric animals such as the ground sloth, stag moose, giant peccaries, and armadillos lived in Missouri. Saber-toothed cats and giant lions were also believed to have roamed Missouri.

k
K

Show me an L
and we'll look for some lead
in mines so dark and deep.
Each day with our picks
we'll chop the black ore,
a hard way to earn our keep.

Missouri produces approximately 85% of the lead in the United States. Shafts take miners down deep into the earth where they blast and dig the ore, forming cavernous rooms called stopes. At first, wagons of ore were hauled by mules who lived their entire lives in the mines. Now, engines pull cars of ore on tracks.

Lead ore comes from galena, our state mineral. After it is mined, it is crushed and smelted to form lead, a heavy metal.

Did you know that Mozarkite, with its pretty pink and purple swirls is our state rock? We even have a state fossil called the crinoid. It was a plant-like animal that lived 250 million years ago when Missouri was covered by water.

How many different types of jobs do these miners have?

L1

L

The mule is the offspring of a male donkey and a female horse. It is Missouri's state animal. Many mules were brought to Missouri when the Santa Fe Trail opened. When Missourians realized the usefulness of this strong and hard-working animal, they became the world leader in producing mules, and the term "Missouri mule" became famous. Mules were used in many ways. Mules pulled wagons of freight to the frontier. They also worked on farms and in mines. Hundreds of thousands of Missouri mules were shipped overseas to haul military equipment in World War I and World War II. Today, mules continue to be used as work animals and for recreational riding.

Mules will follow directions and work very hard. However, mules have the reputation of being very stubborn; they refuse to do things they don't want to do. Many feel that mules are just being smart. They are very cautious and will not cooperate until they are sure of the situation.

Show me an M
and we'll harness the mules,
strong-willed characters and friends.
With ears pointed proudly,
they promise with their bray
to work hard until the day ends.

Native Americans lived in Missouri for thousands of years before Christopher Columbus made his voyage to America. The first inhabitants were nomadic, moving around in search of food. Over time, they learned to plant crops of beans, squash, and corn, allowing them to settle in villages.

About 1,500 years ago, the people of the Mississippian culture built towns along the Mississippi and Missouri Rivers. They are sometimes called Mounds Indians because they built huge earthen mounds in their towns, which were sometimes surrounded by stockade fences and moats. The chief lived on the biggest mound. Their religious practices included carving picture symbols of sunbursts, snakes, and thunderbirds in rock outcroppings. These "petroglyphs" can still be seen.

Can you find boys playing *chunky*? They are throwing spears, trying to hit a flat, circular stone as it rolls.

Show me an N
and we'll meet Native Americans
who lived here long ago.
They traveled the rivers
and built huge mounds
while watching their gardens grow.

The Ozarks cover most of southern Missouri. These rounded mountains form deep hollows, narrow valleys, and long ridges. Beautiful views can be seen from treeless mountain balds. Clear waterways, including the Ozark National Scenic Riverways, twist through the forest and past cliffs. There are many caves, natural bridges, and arches. Names such as Devil's Backbone, Devil's Honeycomb, and Devil's Tollgate suggest the ruggedness of the Ozark landscape.

The name "Ozark" probably came from the French words "aux arcs" which is pronounced the same way. However, no one knows exactly what was meant by these words. Some feel that it meant "with bows," because the native inhabitants were known for their bows. Others feel that it was a shortened way to talk about the area "to the Arkansas," referring to the Arkansas River in the southern part of the mountains. Whatever the meaning, Missourians love the Ozarks' rugged beauty.

Black bears, which had disappeared from the Ozarks, are now beginning to return.

Show me an O
and we'll discover the Ozarks,
following hollows and natural bridges.
Climb up on a bald
to watch the sun set
as fog settles in between ridges.

Pp

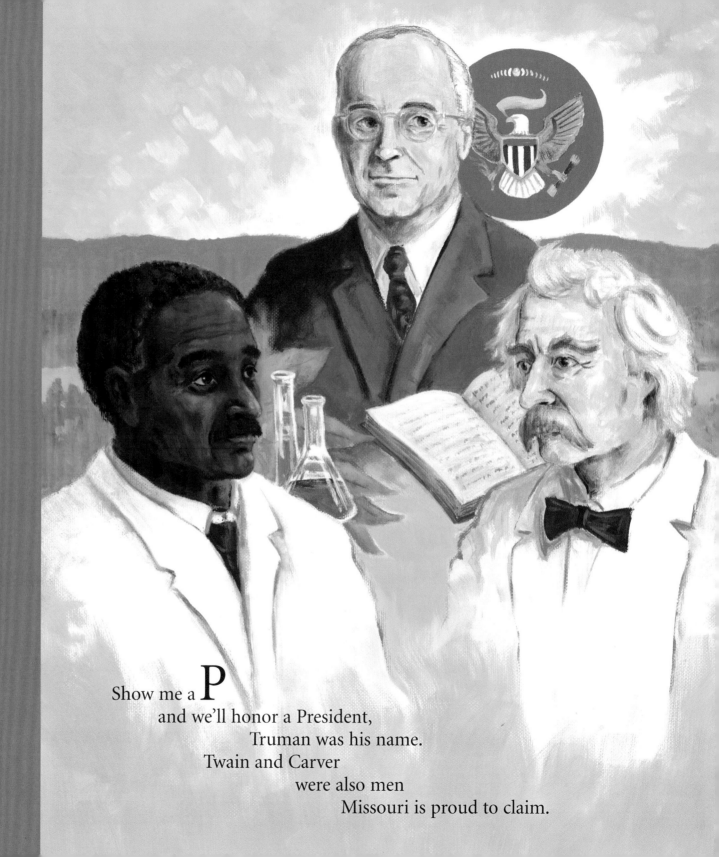

Harry S. Truman, the only president from Missouri, was born in Lamar but lived most of his life in Independence. In 1945, when President Roosevelt died while in office, Vice President Truman became the United States' 33rd president.

Mark Twain was an author who grew up in Hannibal. Two of his most famous books, *The Adventures of Tom Sawyer* and *The Adventures of Huckleberry Finn*, tell stories of boys who grew up along the Mississippi River.

George Washington Carver was born a slave on a Missouri farm near Diamond. His owners, the Carvers, gave him his name and taught him to read and write. George loved to learn, especially about plants. Freed after the Civil War, George left the Carvers at age 10 so he could go to school. After graduating from high school and college, he became a scientist who helped farmers grow better crops. He is famous for discovering 300 ways to use peanuts, including, best of all, peanut butter.

Show me a P
and we'll honor a President,
Truman was his name.
Twain and Carver
were also men
Missouri is proud to claim.

The strongest earthquakes recorded in North America were the New Madrid (pronounced MAD-rid) Earthquakes, which started suddenly on December 16, 1811. In 13 weeks, over 1,800 shocks were counted; so severe they could be felt in the eastern states. The earth shook violently as groundwaves rose and fell. Fissures cracked the earth as large areas of land sank up to 50 feet. The moving earth made thundering noises as buildings were destroyed and forests toppled. Lightning and black sulphur clouds filled the sky. Geysers spit sand, water, and black shale. "Sand boils," like quicksand, were formed.

The Mississippi River was also affected by the quakes. It churned chaotically, rising and plummeting as riverbanks collapsed. Hundreds of trees filled the river. Giant whirlpools, called "sucks," formed. Islands sank. The river changed its course, swallowing the town of New Madrid, and for a while, even ran backwards.

Show me a Q
 and we'll feel the earth quake
 when New Madrid was set in motion.
The earth shook and trembled
 with a fearsome roar
 and land rolled like waves of an ocean.

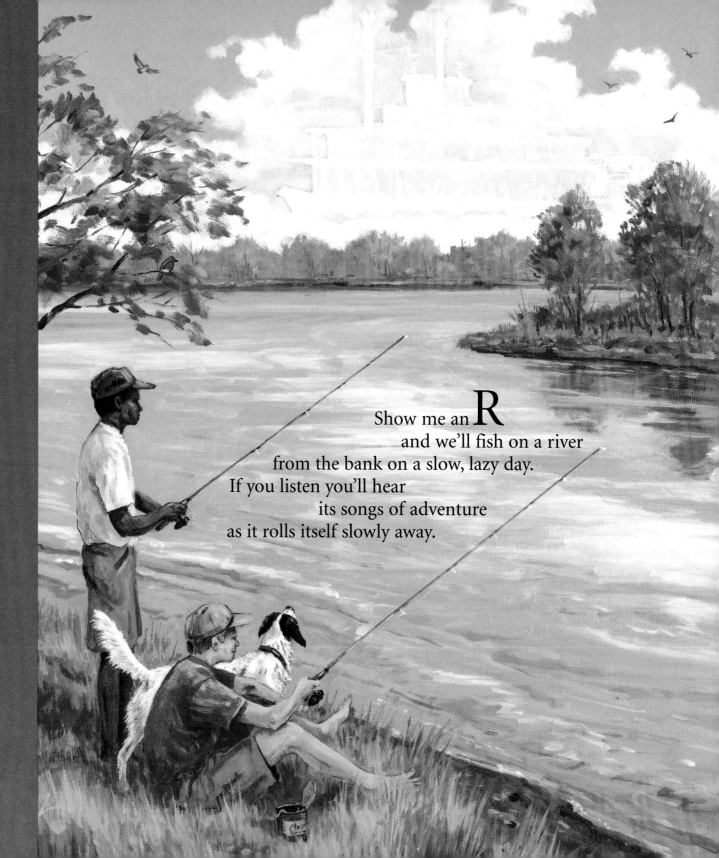

Missouri is a land of rivers. The Mississippi River borders most of the eastern edge of the state. The Missouri River runs along the northwest border and then cuts across the state from Kansas City to St. Louis, where it empties into the Mississippi. Our history is filled with stories connecting us with these mighty rivers, the two largest in North America. Our state's name even has a connection, meaning "people of big canoes."

The great rivers support a variety of wildlife including the channel catfish, Missouri's state fish and a favorite catch for fishermen. An unusual fish, the paddlefish, is Missouri's state aquatic animal. This fish, whose skeleton is made of cartilage, not bone, dates back millions of years. It has a long, spoon-shaped bill and grows up to six feet long.

Wouldn't it have been fun to travel the rivers on a steamboat and watch the water fall from the big paddle wheels?

Show me an R
and we'll fish on a river
from the bank on a slow, lazy day.
If you listen you'll hear
its songs of adventure
as it rolls itself slowly away.

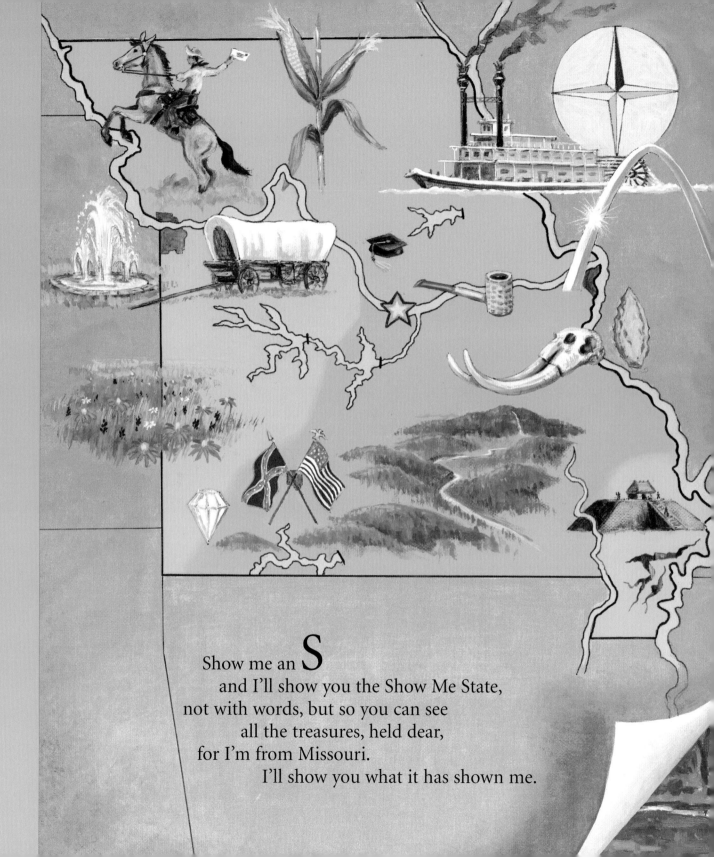

Missouri's nickname, which is written on car license plates, is the Show Me State. The nickname was made famous by a congressman, Willard Duncan Vandiver. During a speech, he said, "I am from Missouri. You have got to show me." It expresses that people from Missouri are cautious and not willing to be fooled by the words of others. They like to see something done rather than hear about it.

With this map, I'll let you "show me" the state of Missouri. Using the pictographs, can you show me the highest point in Missouri? You are right. It is Taum Sauk Mountain. From this 1,772-foot mountain, Mina Sauk Falls, Missouri's tallest falls, tumbles 132 feet. Can you show me the boot heel? The lowest point in the state, at 230 feet above sea level, is on the St. Francis River in the boot heel. Can you show me the northern glacial plains, the southern Ozarks, the western plains, and the Mississippi lowlands?

Can you use the pictographs on the map to show me other places described in this book?

Show me an S
and I'll show you the Show Me State,
not with words, but so you can see
all the treasures, held dear,
for I'm from Missouri.
I'll show you what it has shown me.

Tt

Show me a T
and we'll hike down a trail
pretending that we're pioneers.
We'll discover a forest
or a wild mountain stream,
and maybe see turkeys or deer.

Missouri was the starting point of many famous trails. In 1821, the Santa Fe Trail route was first traveled, starting at Franklin, a town on the Missouri River. A few years later, flooding forced the trailhead to be moved to Independence, which also became the starting point for the Oregon and California Trails. This town bustled with the activity of loading wagons full of all the supplies needed for the long trips west.

Trails continue to be important to Missourians. Missouri's Mark Twain National Forests are filled with trails for hikers and horseback riders who love to experience the quiet beauty of the wilderness. The Ozark Trail, a rugged 500-mile foot trail, is partially completed. Missouri is also the home of the Katy Trail, the nation's longest rail-to-trail project. The 238-mile long Katy Trail State Park was once a railroad bed. Now hikers and bicyclists can travel across the state, seeing views of the Missouri River and its bluffs or passing through forests, rolling farmland, and historic towns.

Show me a U
          and we'll crawl underground
down on our hands and knees.
              Here, blind cave fish live
where day's always night
                  and brown bats fly with ease.

An underground wilderness exists in over 5,600 caves of Missouri. Caves form as limestone is dissolved by water moving underground through cracks in the rock. Cave explorers, called spelunkers, see beautiful cave formations made from mineral deposits. Stalactites, like icicles, hang "tight" from the ceiling. Stalagmites are "mighty" mounds on the floor. Some formations look like rock waterfalls, bacon strips, or flowers.

Near cave entrances, in the twilight zone, many animals find shelter but leave to find food. One is the bat, a nocturnal, flying mammal that eats insects and sleeps hanging upside down. By using echolocation—bouncing noises off cave walls to guide it—the bat can also enter the dark zone. In the dark zone, there is no light. Animals that live their entire lives there are blind. Cave crayfish, grotto salamanders, and blind Ozark cave fish can survive only in the dark zone, where the temperature is always 56-60 degrees. Because plants can't grow without light, cave animals feed on debris brought in by water as well as bat droppings, called guano, which contain undigested insects.

Can you point out which are stalactites and which are stalagmites?

uU

Show me a V
and we'll go on vacation
to Kansas City where fountains flow.
Sun sparkles the water
as it splashes and sprays
a wet and glittery show.

An interesting place to take a vacation is Kansas City, known as the City of Fountains. It has over 200 fountains, more than any city in the world except Rome. Water sprays high in the air, splashing playfully on large bronze sculptures of rearing horses, Roman gods, chariots pulled by seahorses, and dolphins leaping out of pools.

Also on your vacation, you could go to the American Royal, one of the largest combined horse and livestock show and rodeo in the country. You may also visit the world's largest underground business complex. It is built under Kansas City where limestone was quarried a century ago. The Groundhog Run, the world's only underground 10K road race, is held every February.

In its early days, Kansas City was a center for stockyards and rail traffic. Cowboys drove their cattle to Kansas City to be sent east on trains. Kansas City became famous for its beef and continues to be second in the country for rail traffic.

Show me a W
    and we'll gather some walnuts
        in the shade of a tree in the fall.
With our hands stained brown,
    we'll crack open the shells,
        then make candy and cookies for all.

The black walnut, Missouri's state nut, is delicious in ice cream, candy, and baked goods. Missouri's wildlife also enjoys its sweet taste. Walnut trees grow in small groves throughout Missouri.

You can always tell when someone has been picking walnuts because their hands will be stained by the walnut's green husk. Pioneers boiled the husk to make a yellow dye. It is also used for paint. Inside the husk is a hard shell. When ground up, it's used in metal cleansers that clean jet engines, in gas mask filters, as dynamite filler, and to help drill oil wells.

Not only is the nut an important aspect of the walnut tree, but the tree is used for lumber. Missouri is the leading state for production of this dark wood that makes beautiful cabinets and furniture and is also strong enough for gunstocks.

Who would like to enjoy these tasty walnuts?

Would you like to have been a rider for the Pony Express? On April 3, 1860, Johnny Fry, the first Pony Express rider, left a cheering crowd as he rode a horse named Sylph out of St. Joseph carrying mail that would reach San Francisco, California 10 days later. Johnny was one of a team of relay riders. Each Pony Express rider carried a "mochila," a saddlebag that held the mail. The rider would race 20 or 30 miles to a relay station where he would stop for less than 2 minutes and then gallop off on a fresh horse. Then he would ride to the next relay station. After he had covered approximately 100 miles, the mochila would be handed over to a new rider who would take over the route. This kept the mail going day and night.

Riders had to be strong and tough, riding in rain or shine. They faced many dangers including scorched deserts, flooded rivers, quicksand, mountain blizzards, and robbers. The excitement of the Pony Express lasted only 19 months due to the completion of the transcontinental telegraph.

What animals does the Pony Express rider gallop by in the picture?

X X

Show me an X
and we'll ride for the Pony Express
with galloping hooves and flying tail.
We'll race across rivers,
through mountains and plains
to quickly deliver the mail.

Yy

Show me a **Y**
and we'll paint the state yellow
with sunny skies and amber wheat.
We'll take a hayride
down gold-leafed lanes
and have corn-on-the-cob to eat.

If Missouri were to have a state color, it might be yellow. Missouri's farmlands are brushed with this vivid hue. Sunny-faced wild flowers dot summer fields. Yellow leaves paint fall forests and wheat fields wave their golden heads. Bales of amber hay dot the country-side, ready to feed beef cattle, which Missouri is second in the nation for raising.

Bright yellow mountains of corn, one of Missouri's major crops, are harvested to feed livestock, or used to make breakfast cereal. Corn syrup and corn oil are frequent ingredients in many foods, such as ketchup, margarine, candy, and soda pop. One unusual use for corn is the corncob pipe. Nearly all corncob pipes in the world are made in Washington, MO. Many famous people, including poet Carl Sandburg, President Ford, President Eisenhower, General MacArthur, and Missouri's General Pershing had a corncob pipe from Missouri. Corn is best, however, when you sink your teeth into a sweet yellow ear of corn-on-the-cob that drips with golden butter.

Do you see where this bluebird lives?

Show me a Z
        and together we'll zoom
                through the air and into space.
                        Our minds take flight
                                and imaginations soar
                                        as into the future we race.

Missouri has played a part in man's dream of zooming through the skies and out into space. In the early 1900s, St. Louis hosted the first international balloon race, the first dirigible meet, and the first international aviation meet. In 1927, Charles Lindbergh became the first to fly nonstop across the Atlantic Ocean. He named his plane "The Spirit of St. Louis" in honor of the St. Louis businessmen who supported his flight.

Missouri helped the United States move into the space age. The *Mercury* and *Gemini* spacecrafts were made by McDonnell Aircraft in St. Louis. The *Mercury* spacecraft carried Alan Shepard, Jr., the first American in space and John Glenn, Jr., the first American to orbit the Earth. On the *Gemini* missions, the first space walks occurred and, for the first time, two spacecraft met and docked together out in space.

The Hubble Space Telescope was named after Edwin Hubble from Marshfield. This astronomer confirmed the idea that there are billions of galaxies and that they are moving apart. With the Hubble Space Telescope, astronomers can zoom in on these galaxies far, far away.

Zz

Show Me Some ABC Questions About Missouri.

A. A steamboat sank in the Missouri River leaving its entire cargo covered with mud. It was dug up 130 years later. What was the name of this steamboat?

B. After the Civil War, a violent vigilante group decided to take the law into their own hands. They got their name from their secret meeting spot. Do you know what they were called and why?

C. What is the name of the nation's first suburban shopping center planned for automobile traffic?

D. A famous cartoonist was raised on a farm near Marceline, MO, where he sold his first sketches at the age of seven. Who was he?

E. What Missourian, born in Hannibal, played the voice for Disney's cartoon character Jiminy Cricket?

F. What organization has sent thousands of children to Kansas City each year since the 1920s to learn about farming and farm animals at its annual convention?

G. What U.S. President built a farm near St. Louis named "Hardscrabble?"

H. What sport does the St. Louis Blues play?

I. In 1946, former British Prime Minister Sir Winston Churchill spoke at Westminster College in Fulton, MO. What was the nickname given to his famous speech?

J. What were the names of two notorious outlaw brothers who robbed many banks and trains in Missouri?

K. Which Missouri city has the largest population?

L. The oldest reservoir west of the Mississippi River got its name from Taney County, MO, where its dam was built. Can you guess the name of this man-made lake?

M. A famous Missourian author took his pen name from a river term used to measure the depth of the water. When this term was called out, it meant the boat was in two fathoms, or 12 feet, of water. Do you know the river term?

N. Some of these are Clever or Peculiar. You may scream Eureka, but you won't win a Diamond for a prize from a Tightwad. Can you figure out this riddle?

O. What was the name of a large Indian tribe whose cultural and political center was located in Missouri?

P. At one time, one-third of Missouri was covered with this. Can you guess what it was?

Q. What is a nickname for Springfield, the largest city in the Ozarks?

R. From the 1920s to the 1960s, America's "main street" crossed through Missouri on its 2,200-mile trek from Chicago to Los Angeles. What was this famous "main street" called?

S. Where was Missouri's capitol from 1821 to 1826 before it was moved to Jefferson City?

T. The Cherokee Indians were forced by federal troops to leave the eastern states. In 1838, they crossed the Mississippi River into Missouri on their way farther west to "Indian Territory." What was the name given to their trail?

U. What is the name of the first state university west of the Mississippi River? It was founded in 1839.

V. Many grapes are grown in Missouri. What are places that grow grapes called?

W. In 1985, the Kansas City Royals beat the St. Louis Cardinals, four games to three. In what series were they playing?

X. Harry Truman was staying at this place in 1948 when he learned that he had won the presidential election. Many others have visited this place to drink and bathe in its mineral waters. What place is this?

Y. In 1788, the crew of ten boats joined together, going up the Mississippi River to St. Louis to rid the river of pirates. What was this called?

Z. There are three zoos in Missouri. Do you know their names and where they are?

Answers

A. Arabia.

B. Baldknobbers, because they met on a bald mountain knob in the Ozarks.

C. Country Club Plaza, in Kansas City.

D. Walt Disney.

E. Cliff Edwards, also known as Ukelele Ike.

F. Future Farmers of America.

G. President Ulysses S. Grant, our 18th president.

H. Hockey.

I. The Iron Curtain Speech.

J. Jesse and Frank James.

K. Kansas City.

L. Lake Taneycomo.

M. (Mark) twain.

N. Names of some Missouri towns.

O. Osage.

P. Prairie.

Q. Queen City of the Ozarks.

R. Route 66.

S. St. Charles.

T. Trail of Tears.

U. University of Missouri.

V. Vineyards.

W. The World Series.

X. Excelsior Springs.

Y. Year of the Ten Boats.

Z. St. Louis Zoo, Swope Park Zoo in Kansas City, and Dickerson Park Zoo in Springfield.

Judy Young and Ross B. Young

Judy Young is a speech and language pathologist, and an award-winning poet. She works with elementary children, helping them to understand and use language. She encourages children to write by reading poetry and discussing it in the classroom. Her fascination with words and love of language is evidenced by numerous published pieces in literary journals and magazines. Judy received a Master of Arts in Speech and Language Pathology at the University of Tulsa in 1980.

The art of Ross B. Young is often associated with paintings of the world's greatest sporting dogs. Ross has been a professional artist since he received his Master of Arts in Painting from the University of Tulsa in 1980. His artwork has been displayed in national and international art shows, galleries, and museums, and on the covers of many magazines and books. Ross regularly shares his expertise and love of art with children at local elementary schools.

Judy and Ross Young live in the country near Springfield, MO. They have a daughter, Brett, a son, Reid, and five dogs. *S is for Show Me: A Missouri Alphabet* is their first children's book.